DO I HAVE TO?

It's never too early
or too late to make
your plan!
Be Blessed!
Sheri Wilson

DO I HAVE TO?

SHERI A. WILSON

Clovercroft/Publishing

Do I Have To?

Published by Clovercroft Publishing, Franklin, Tennessee

Illustrated by Jacob Warhop

Edited by Emily Zoscak

Cover Design by Erik Trent

Interior Design by Suzanne Lawing

Printed in the United States of America

978-1-945507-80-9

Dedicated to my parents Bill and Jeanette Perich
For providing all that I needed to build a
strong foundation in life. For the commitment
to raise us to know and love God, and for the wisdom
of your experience you've shared over the years.

And to my children, Katie, Mike, and Sam.
I hope and pray I passed on to you the importance
of knowing and loving God, the nuggets of wisdom
I learned from my parents, and the bits of
wisdom I've learned as I walk my own path.
May yours be as blessed as mine.

CONTENTS

INTRO

Economics. It's a class that many of you took in high school where teachers taught the basics of finance. While having learned about things like scarcity, opportunity-cost, investments, and cost-benefit analyses as they relate to large economic entities is important, it likely did not fully prepare you to manage your own finances. This book is here to change that.

If you are reading to discover how to properly manage your money—great! You're already ahead of many of your peers. If you are consulting this book for advice on how to manage a loved one's finances, maybe your child's or grandchild's, it is important to remember this: if those you care for are not financially independent, then their financial stability depends on someone, or something, else. This might be their parent(s), other loved ones, or even credit cards. No matter their age, it is imperative that they develop a spending plan that sets them up for success and prevents them from hindering yours.

Where do you find such a plan? The answer is here in these very pages. I wrote this book specifically to teach young adults and their loved ones the personal financial planning fundamentals that were not always taught in the classroom. In order to stay out of debt and save for the future, it is essential that you know how to correctly manage your money. Especially in today's world, where there are always new credit cards you can open to "pay" for things, fancy programs for purchase that "manage" your finances, and other quick fixes that claim to make sound decisions about where you should allocate your hard-earned cash. While these things *sound* great, they will likely not provide you with a full understanding of the fundamentals you need in order to build a strong financial foundation.

Creating a spending plan that keeps you out of debt while also allowing you to meet your needs is something that only *you* can do correctly. You need to be the one deciding where your money goes. If you are not, then you could wind up creating unnecessary financial problems for yourself down the line. Trust me when I say being in debt is not fun. Unlike the picture of struggle Hollywood and other artists sometimes glamorize, there is nothing desirable about being a slave to moneylenders and/or living paycheck to paycheck.

The fact is, living in the modern world is expensive. Financial commitments are necessary. Each month, you must pay for necessities like rent, utilities, insurance, transportation, student loans, groceries, and then you'll want to buy fun things! You spend money on a lot more than you think each month!

When it comes to these necessary living expenses, it is common to wonder, possibly aloud with a heavy sigh, "Do I have to pay for all of these things?" The answer is a resounding YES; you absolutely do! The reality is that as an adult, you are expected to make good on your financial commitments. The opportunity to decide how you live your life also comes with the responsibility of footing the bill for it.

Paying for your expenses while also enjoying the freedom you dreamed about growing up requires you to put financial structure into your life. I was lucky enough to learn this from my parents and will share the fundamentals that they taught me in these pages.

My father is a member of what many have called the "Greatest Generation:" those who grew up during the Great Depression. Folks born in this era know the true meaning of sacrifice. They worked hard every single day to provide their families with food on the table and clothing on their backs—things that many of us who are unfamiliar with such struggles easily take for granted.

Growing up during the Great Depression taught my parents valuable lessons in discipline and money allocation. They were kind enough to share many of these lessons with my husband and me as we raised our own children. One such lesson I learned at a family dinner when my children were preschool-aged. We ordered food, and when it arrived we saw that the portions sizes for the kid's meals were twice what my two children could eat. Noticing this, my dad commented, "I'll never be too rich to waste food. Next time, why don't you order a meal for them to split, and then if they want more, order another meal?" As young parents, we didn't even think about it in those terms. We were so focused on making sure that they had something to eat, we did not even stop to consider that we might actually end up ordering too much food, causing the leftovers to go to waste! I believe that was his point. Many of us are lucky enough to live in a state of abundance while going through life on autopilot without thinking about the small ways in which we can save resources. I have thought about that dinner often over the years. My father's words made me think about our lifestyle, and his wisdom inspired a change in how I view money.

I hope that in sharing my experience and financial know-how, this book is able to be that inspiration for you. I am a woman of faith who values those who came before her. In the following pages, I will refer to stories from my past and Bible verses that have shaped my perspective on money, using scriptural references to emphasize certain lessons. Additionally, I have worked in finance for seven years helping people of all ages and backgrounds achieve success in managing their money. I know that by sharing a lot of what I have learned in this book, I can help you too.

I know that it's not always fun to crunch the numbers and allocate your income, but it does not have to be tedious either. This book is meant to serve as a guide in structuring your finances so you are able to spend your hard-earned cash wisely, stay out of debt, and save for the things you want to accomplish in your lifetime. Start by writing in the Spending Plan, Goals Worksheets, and Net Worth Statement. You will get a complete picture of where you stand financially.

Proverbs 16:9 (NJKV): "A man's heart plans his way but the Lord directs his steps."

Let the desire to achieve your goals serve as motivation to trust the process detailed in these pages. I know that if you follow these guidelines, you will find yourself on the path to financial success. Trust me, in the years to come, you will be thankful that you took several hours of your time now to invest in your future.

CHAPTER ONE

WHAT I NEED — THE BASICS

All right! You're here, an adult at last. How does it feel? After fantasizing about it for years, as a grown up you finally get to call the big shots! Where to live? What to drive? If things like bologna sandwiches and an entire box of macaroni and cheese qualify as acceptable dinner options? (Personal conclusion: they do in moderation.) What being an adult really comes down to is deciding how you're going to spend your hard-earned cash to achieve what you want out of life.

How do you feel about this newly acquired responsibility? If you're anxious, that's okay. It's natural to be a bit apprehensive when beginning to lay the foundation of your financial life. Not many people truly know how to create and maintain a spending plan that allows them financial freedom: free of spending-related stress, free to save up for a relaxing beach vacation or that luxury sports car, and free to easily accommodate last-minute life expenses like major repairs or medical emergencies.

If you're less than thrilled, that's normal, too. Surely there are plenty of other things you would rather be doing than taking precious free time out of your already jam-packed schedule to think about finances. It's not fun to pay bills, especially when you'd rather use your hard-earned money to buy that new pair of shoes or those tickets to your favorite band's concert.

If you're excited to create your plan, that's the spirit! It really is thrilling to be in control of where your money's going. You get to give yourself one of the best, most desired gifts out there: long-term financial stability, which is a relief quite like no other. Worrying about where your next rent check, or heck, even meal, is coming from is an unfortunate reality that many around the world struggle with. It's empowering to set yourself up so that you never have to grapple with that burden.

To do this you first have to learn how to create a financially sound, personal spending plan (normally called a budget) based on your income. If you choose to forgo this foundation, your financial life will crumble under the weight of your needs and wants due to an inadequate support structure. Nobody wants that! Thus, you must start with the basics.

Principles

The Merriam-Webster dictionary defines "princi-ples" as "rules or codes of conduct." Essentially, principles are ideals and behaviors that you consider valuable and worthy of embodying.

A few examples of principles people can live by

- Honesty
- Integrity
- Trustworthiness
- Helpfulness
- Patience
- Kindness
- Generosity
- Lovingness
- Thoughtfulness
- Obedience
- Respectability
- Unselfishness

As you begin this intimate relationship with your personal finances, it's imperative to get in touch with your individual principles. They define who you are as a person. Your principles act like the rebar in a cement foundation for every decision you make, whether it is how much money to spend, where to shop, or how to interact with others.

You will establish these values throughout your life, gaining some and losing others as you experience the world around you. Your family, friends, employers, and community all contribute to your perspective on what a desirable life looks like, as do your upbringing, faith, and current circumstances. These beliefs shape who you are and how you participate as a member of your family, your community, your nation, and your world.

How does all of this play into money? Simple. Your principles determine what is important to you, thereby influencing where you choose to spend your hard-earned money.

A few examples of how principles affect where people spend their money

- People who value learning might spend money on educational endeavors, subscriptions to news sources, and books.

- People who have integrity will make it a priority to honor their commitments, such as quickly paying back a loan or their share of something.

- People who value nice things might spend their income on a fancy car and brand-name clothes.

- People who value giving are more likely to donate part of their earnings on donations to places of worship, charities, and those in need.

While principles don't implicitly have ties to money, they definitely factor into where you decide to spend your dollars. Let's say you have a little extra money in this month's paycheck. Will you deposit it into a vacation savings account or splurge on a new outfit for work? Will you utilize it to pay down your student loans this month or donate the extra money to your favorite charity? Will you save it towards your future home or choose to buy that super sleek end table you didn't *need*, but that looks absolutely fantastic by your couch? It should be noted that there isn't a wrong option for any of these decisions. Your money is just that, yours, and *you* get to decide where to spend it.

That being said, it's important to check in with yourself often to make sure you are not betraying who you are by compromising your principles. Navigating decisions in life requires being in touch with what's important to you, financial and otherwise. Be honest with yourself. What matters to you? Not the latest style trend, your crush, your parents, your best friend, but *you*. That's not to say their opinions aren't important, but you are the one who has to live with the decisions you make. If you are not honest about what you value most, you are never going to be truly happy. And that's the truth!

Stewardship

Perfecting your financial plan isn't going to happen overnight. It's going to take time, reflection, and patience. It's going to take an understanding of **stewardship**, or the "the careful and responsible management of something entrusted to one's care," as defined by the Merriam-Webster dictionary.

A common example of stewardship relates to extracurricular activities. Growing up, many of you participated in classes and programs outside of your core studies that piqued your, or let's be honest, your parent's interest. You spent your afternoons engaged in school sports, clubs, the fine arts, and more. When first learning these activities, you were not immediately an expert. No. It took time to learn the fundamentals—dribbling and setting the ball, learning how to read music, the art of blending colors, and when to apply essential formulas. Through experience, you became proficient in these activities by slowly advancing your skills over time. You embraced your natural desire to learn more about the things that brought you joy and success. You can bet Michael Jordan and Adele didn't become legends without putting in the work to master all aspects of their craft, both basic and advanced.

This same idea of learning the basics, developing the experience, and progressing to mastery applies to your finances. You must entrust yourself to take the tools you learn in this book and use them to create long-term financial success. It will not happen overnight, but as time advances so will your income allocation experience and thus, your financial freedom.

As the Lord said in his teachings in the Parable of the Talents:

Matthew 25:21 (NKJV): "Well done, good and faithful servant; you were faithful over a few things, I will make you ruler over many things. Enter into the joy of your Lord."

The majority of people who suddenly find themselves with a fortune often fail to create a plan that allows them to keep it. Not knowing the fundamentals of how to handle a large sum of money, they quickly spend their winnings and fall into debt.

Learn from their mistakes. Don't overindulge. Instead, master the basics, create a spending plan, and stick with it. Stay in tune with your finances. If you do, in time, you'll be granted the freedom to enjoy a lifestyle that makes you truly happy.

Applying What You Know

You have a plethora of knowledge at your fingertips. Literally! If you want to learn about anything under the sun, you need only to go to your computer, laptop, tablet, or phone and enter a topic into a search engine. Within seconds, you have more material than you could ever need on that subject.

There is a difference between knowing things and actually applying those things to your life for the better. You have access to so much information, but are you using this intel to make wise decisions?

Technology today has trained those of us living in the Western world to expect near instant gratification in almost every aspect of our lives. Things such as texting, same-day shipping, and video-streaming services have conditioned us to want and then get something at practically the same time. Human connection? It happens with just a few taps on a screen. Want a new pair of headphones? You can buy them with one click! Itching to see the latest blockbuster? Press a few buttons on your remote and voilà, the opening credits are rolling.

In an age where instant gratification is the norm, it's often hard to fathom taking the time to cultivate a financial plan suited to your specific needs. Isn't it much easier to not think about it at all and just spend? You can find apps and websites that will generate this kind of plan for you in a matter of seconds, but they aren't asking you what is important to help you find the value in the income you earn.

Another problem with these plans and apps is that none of them are specifically suited to you and your needs. Everyone has different goals and income. Meaning, you need to create a spending plan that works for you.

> **Knowledge**—information, know-how, and facts a person gains through education or experience.

> **Wisdom**—the ability to make a decision based on previous experience, understanding, and intuition.

In short, wisdom is knowledge applied. When someone asks me for advice and I give it, I hear the answer "I know" all too frequently. I know that *you know* the information. What I am suggesting is that you apply that knowledge to your decisions about money and about your life. Don't just know it. Use what you know. Get it? Show that you know by the way you live your life: debt free, within your means.

Money, Money, Money

Now that the importance of becoming well versed in the fundamentals and applying this knowledge to your own financial life have been established, here are some definitions that are essential to know before starting your own spending plan.

First up, what the heck is a *spending plan*?

Spending Plan—a financial structure, personal to

you, that dictates how you allocate your income. This structure takes into account things like your principles, assets, and liabilities. Spending plans will change over time as life's priorities shift.

Here are some other helpful definitions to help you better navigate your finances:

Rules of Thumb—guidance derived from the experiences and practices of others, not theories.

Assets *(what you have)*—the large ticket items that you own. This includes items such as your house, cars, rental properties, collectable coins, art, jewelry, savings accounts, investment accounts, checking accounts, cash, etc.

Money—banknotes and coins that society has deemed valuable. You exchange these entities for goods and services.

Taxes—a monetary contribution to state revenue required of all US citizens. The amount that you pay varies based on location, income, property value, etc.

Earned Income—what you get paid through working.

Gross Income—total pay you receive for completed work, including employer matching 401(k) contributions, insurance, and additional benefits paid by your employer. These are pre-tax earnings.

Net Income—considered your "take-home pay,"

this is the total amount you receive after deductions for 401(k) contributions, taxes, insurance, and benefits. Essentially, it's what's deposited into your bank account each pay period.

Savings—the amount of money you save over time after paying all of your necessary expenses. These funds should be deposited into at least two separate bank accounts:

| *Emergency Savings*—money used for last minute, unexpected expenses (e.g., repairs or medical bills). Having six months of living expenses saved up is a good rule to live by.

2 *Goals Savings*—funds used for short and long-term goals you will establish in chapter 2. Depending on the size of your goals and how much time you have to accomplish them, you could have separate savings accounts for your (a) bigger aspirations (owning a house, having a wedding, taking an expensive vacation, retirement) and another for your smaller ones (pur (b) chasing a couch, seeing your favorite band in concert, etc.).

Liabilities *(what you owe, debt)*—anything of monetary value that you owe to someone else that must be paid back (e.g., credit card loans, car loans, home loans, student loans, personal loans owed to family or friends).

Credit Card—an unsecured loan with a steep interest rate.

Net Worth (assets minus liabilities)—the monetary difference between what you own and what you owe. If you sold all your possessions in addition to paying off all of your debts, how much cash would you have in your hot little hand? Would that number be positive or negative?

Cash Flow—your incoming and outgoing funds, in essence the revolving door of your bank accounts.

> *Incoming funds*—these include deposits into your accounts (your paycheck, a birthday check from Grandma, that money your friend owes you for last week's lunch, etc.).

> *Outgoing funds*—are anything withdrawn from your account (monthly living expenses, date night movie tickets, contributions to a savings account, etc.).

> *Checking Account*—a bank account that allows withdrawals and deposits of checks.

> *Savings Account*—a bank account that earns interest on the amount of money inside of it.

Living Expenses—the amount of money you need to live as a functional member of society and pay for things like rent, a car, utilities, doctor appointments, insurance, etc.

Lifestyle Expenses—costs related to funding your immediate wants (seeing movies, eating out, buying clothes) as well as short- and long-term goals (purchasing a TV, traveling, having a wedding).

Giving—monetary donations to charitable causes, places of worship, or to those in need. You can also make material donations and give your time; however, when making your spending plan you only need to focus on your monetary gifts.

Now that you understand the basic building blocks of personal finance, it's time to create spending plan targeted on accomplishing your life's goals.

Luke 12:15 (NKJV) "And He said to them, "Take heed and beware of covetousness, for one's life does not consist in the abundance of the things he possesses.""

As this verse from The Bible implies, during and after this process it is key to stay on course and not fall victim to greed. There are greater values in life than things and money. In chapter 2, you will determine what these things are for you.

_____

_____

_____

_____

_____

_____

_____

_____

_____

_____

_____

_____

_____

_____

_____

_____

_____

_____

_____

_____

_____

_____

_____

_____

_____

_____

_____

CHAPTER TWO

WHAT I WANT – GOALS AND LIFESTYLE

What's one thing that everybody has in common? Everyone make decisions. Sure, they're about different things. However, the point is that life is full of decisions. Easy and difficult. Large and small. Many of them can greatly affect your finances.

Previously, you learned about principles and the need to determine what is important to you. This chapter is all about learning how to take these core beliefs into consideration when making important life decisions and setting goals.

Consistently Making Good Decisions

In physics, you likely learned about Sir Isaac Newton's third law: every action has an equal and opposite reaction. This is also true of decisions. Every decision that you make has a consequence—some good and some bad. When forced to stop and think about decisions and how their consequences may affect you, you will likely make better choices. When you think about how your decisions can affect you financially, you *really* start to change the way you make them. For every decision, especially financial ones, it's imperative to ask yourself what the best choice is for you that will help you accomplish your goals.

Let's take a minute and talk about emotional decisions. Many of your decisions are made on an emotional level or based on how you feel. For instance, some people go shopping because they want to make themselves feel better. More times than not, this leads to buyer's remorse. Usually, emotional decisions such as this are made quickly because it is human nature to want to feel better fast. Sometimes, the emotions are fear-based. Fear Of Missing Out, a.k.a., FOMO, is a real thing. The idea of missing out on a terrific sale can cause you to make an irrational financial decision in the moment. Frequently falling victim to FOMO can cause harmful effects to your bank account. Hastily made or poorly planned decisions that carry little to no long-term benefit to your financial situation only provide a short-term boost to your happiness level. That is why you must consistently make an effort to base your decisions and spending on logic, not emotion. Going forward, pause before you buy something you don't need and consider the consequences.

Proverbs 21:5 (NKJV): "The plans of the diligent

lead surely to plenty. But those of everyone who is hasty, surely to poverty."

Setting Your Goals and Deciding What's Important

When it comes to deciding what you want to achieve in life, many possibilities come to mind. The many decisions can feel overwhelming at times. While this is totally normal, instead of embracing that discomfort head-on, it is easy to clam up and procrastinate on making these decisions. Even though it might feel a bit scary, it's important to think about what you want to accomplish in your life and when.

When thinking about these things take your time and don't rush the process.

Are there any bucket-list items you hope to check off? Do you value experiences like a dream vacation, or is there an item you would like to buy, like your dream car? What's your definition of a well-lived life? You need to be honest with yourself about what's going to make you happy. Only you can decide what happiness looks like. Many of these goals will require some money to be spent, so you will need to prioritize them and begin saving toward making them happen. The bigger the dollar amount, the more time it will take to save enough money to achieve them. The goal is to stay out of debt while working toward accomplishing your goals in life and learning to pay cash for the goals that require purchases!

Pay Yourself First—Goals and Timing

Paying yourself first means structuring your finances so that with each paycheck, you set aside a little money towards funding your future goals. The goal timeframes described below are recommended for young adults recently graduating from college or shortly thereafter. Before you can begin to pay into your savings account, you must establish a purpose for each dollar. Knowing what your goals are will motivate you to save for them. Planning for a wedding or your retirement may seem a bit premature at any early age, but in order to afford these things when you choose, you must start early.

Structuring Your Goals

Growing up, my dad frequently repeated an unknown's famous quote, "Inch by inch, life's a cinch. Yard by yard, life is hard." The lesson here is to take things slowly. As exciting as it is to think about all of the great things you're going to achieve in your time on Earth, it's key to know that you cannot accomplish them all at once. If you try, you will end up living outside of your means, eventually accruing debt and becoming a slave to creditors. Nobody enjoys this type of lifestyle. Life and your goals within it take time!

One of the best ways to stay on track and avoid falling into debt is to pace your goals, breaking them up into smaller goals and then placing those on a timeline. Let's say you have a goal of starting a garden. An oasis of flowers, herbs, and vegetables isn't simply going to appear in your backyard (or on your windowsill)! First, you'll need to make a plan of what you want the garden to look like. Where will it go? What will you grow? What kind of soil will you use? Will you pot some of the plants, or put them directly in the earth? Next, you'll need to determine what you need to make it happen—the materials, the time commitment, and the funds. Finally, depending on how much you can comfortably save each month and the urgency with which you feel the project needs to be completed, you'll determine a date by which to accomplish your plan. Based on your goal date, you can assign the two previous steps their respective deadlines. If it is January and your goal is to have a garden by June, you may decide to come up with what the garden will look like and what resources it will require by the end of the month. This plan gives you February through May to save up the funding to buy all of the plants. If you decide in April that you need a couple more months to save up, then shift your timeline. However, if the project is really important to you, analyze your spending plan to determine other expenses you can cut back on in order to meet your new goal.

Reaching a goal makes you feel good, as if you are headed in the right direction. Breaking up some of your loftier goals into shorter-term ones you can reach in less time helps you feel motivated to stay on track.

On page 75 there is a worksheet that allows you to list all of your goals, big and small, and then place them on a basic timeline. Feel free to use this resource or get inventive with how you monitor the progress of your goals. Some people like to keep track of theirs in a document online, while others are more creative with it. Goals are merely a dream until they are written down and tracked. Write them down, and they become real! Your goals might also change as time goes on, and that's okay. It's invaluable to have a starting point of accomplishments to work toward. Taking the time to really flesh out the things you want to achieve will make it that much easier to determine where you need to spend (and save!) your money. I know a girl who writes her goals and their steps out on a piece of paper, cuts each step into a separate strip, and pins them onto a cork board timeline above her desk. Having something to look at each week reminds her of her aspirations and causes her to think twice about unnecessary spending. Whatever works for you is how you need to be tracking your goals.

Think about your goals in terms of the increments below. There are examples included to help you know where you should put some of your goals on the worksheet.

Short-term Goals: Six Months to One Year

Pay into a six-month cash reserve to use for emergencies. These may include such things as new tires, replace a washer or dryer, or unforeseen dental or medical expenses. You could even begin to save for the beach vacation that you hope to take next year.

Medium-term Goals: One Year to Three Years

Pay into a down payment on a new car or save for

that month-long tour of Europe. The goal is to pay cash for the vacation, or in the case of the car, lower the amount of money you borrow at an interest rate.

Long-term Goals: Three to Five Years

Save up for a down payment on your first home. A good rule of thumb is to save up enough to pay twenty percent of the home's price up front, in cash.

Ultra-long-term Goals: Five or More Years

Save for the funds to start your own business or for future retirement income.

In doing this exercise, you might be thinking that some of your goals will not influence your bank account. For instance, if you want to learn to cook, you might be able to learn to cook without spending a dime outside of the normal cost of groceries. However, most goals that don't cost you anything right now eventually will. Continuing with the cooking example, as you progress your skills, you may want to take cooking classes or buy new kitchen gadgets. Another good example of this is a wedding. You may be single now, but know that someday you may want to marry. Weddings costs increase every year. While it may be a long-term goal, it's important to keep in mind that if you start saving for your wedding early on, you will have the funds to have the wedding you desire. The lesson here is that you need to save for your long-term goals while also saving for your short-term goals. Saving for your future by following your spending plan is not a sprint. It is a marathon!

Possible Goals
- Getting married
- Having children
- Owning your own home
- Learning a new language
- Traveling the world
- Starting your own business
- Having a library in your house
- Getting another degree
- Living in a big city
- Adopting a dog
- Writing a novel
- Learning to cook
- Starting a garden
- Purchasing a sports car

Rules of Thumb

- It is helpful to revisit your goals so you can gain more perspective on how far you've come. Save each of the worksheets that you complete throughout this book in a file where you can easily refer back to them and see your progress.

- Every decision you make has a consequence—good or bad. Making emotional decisions often leads to poorer choices being made. However, when you take the time to think through your options and make a logical decision, the outcome has a higher likelihood of being beneficial.

- Don't repeat past bad decisions. The outcome is not going to be different; there may be more to lose next time around!

- When establishing your goals, think about things you want to achieve in your lifetime. Write them down!

- To make reaching these goals more manageable, break them down into smaller steps that you can accomplish over time. Place all of your goal steps on a timeline and track your progress in reaching them. Adjust along the way if needed!

- When you reach a goal, be happy and celebrate a couple of things:
    o You changed your spending and saving habits.
    o You showed great discipline seeing this goal to the finish.
    o Reward yourself by buying what you saved for: take the trip, purchase the home, start the business, or retire!

If, however, you reach the goal and change your mind about spending the money—that's okay. Changing your mind may show that what you thought you wanted six months ago isn't as important to you now. Maybe there is something else that you would rather buy. Give yourself permission to change your mind and buy something different or reallocate that money to another goal you would like to reach sooner. The point is, you accomplished saving up for the goal and, by doing that, created choices for yourself. Own that and be proud! Understanding the power you have when you take charge and steward your money properly is so, so very important for you to realize.

_____

_____

_____

_____

_____

_____

_____

_____

_____

_____

_____

_____

_____

_____

_____

_____

_____

_____

_____

_____

_____

_____

_____

_____

_____

_____

CHAPTER THREE

DO I HAVE TO? –
MAKE YOUR PLAN

Despite the best of intentions, it's hard to have success in effectively allocating your money without a little planning and hard work toward doing so. This chapter is all about taking what you've previously learned about the fundamentals of money, your values, making decisions, and goal setting to create an actionable spending plan that works for you.

Current Financial Snapshot

Before creating that plan, it's crucial that you answer certain questions to get a better picture of your financial situation. Getting a grasp on your current spending patterns will help you determine what adjustments you need to make to your current habits.

Let's start with the big picture; your net worth statement. Then we will move on to spending habits.

On page 87 there is a Net Worth Statement worksheet to help you answer the following questions:

- What is your monthly income? Yearly income?

- How much money do you have in your checking account? (Assets)

- How much money do you have in your various savings or investment accounts? (Assets)

- List the property you own. (Assets)

- How much money do you owe people right now? Credit card debt? Loans? (Liabilities)

Assets – Liabilities = Net Worth

Either it is positive or negative. If it's positive, you are on the right track. If it is negative, that means you have too much debt. Answer this question. What do you want your net worth statement to look like? The two ways to influence your net worth statement is to make more money and/or spend less. You have the power to make it better and now is the best time to start. What you do next can determine your future. Take some time and look at your bank statements. How much money did you waste last month on things like fast food? Drinks? Sales at your favorite store? It's okay to spend frivolously occasionally, but how often is occasionally for you? Has it actually become a habit?

When answering these questions, it is important to be honest with yourself. It's okay to learn that each month you currently spend a bit more on fast food and tickets to the local movie theater than you expected. The first step in adjusting your spending habits to save more money is acknowledging that there is room for improvement. Now is not the time to fudge the numbers. Tricking yourself into believing that you are living within your means when you are not only creates more problems down the line. You need to know where you stand financially in order to make the best choices for your future.

Creating Your Spending Plan

To most efficiently spend your money, you need to figure where your money needs to go by creating a personal spending plan. This plan will serve as your guide for spending money throughout the month!

Every last cent of your income should have a purpose, and you are the one who decides that purpose. You should always be the one directing your money where to go. If you currently owe creditors money, you already see how your credit card, student loans, and/or a car payment get first dibs on your paycheck each month. Thus, you are no longer in control of that cash. Those who you owe are. Taking time to create a spending plan that puts structure and balance into your financial life will help you to avoid this situation entirely. That time is now.

You are going to start by organizing your expenses into three lists: *What I Need*, *Do I Have to*, and *What I Want*. Each month, your paycheck will be divided up between the expenses on each list.

There is a Spending Plan worksheet on page 79

43

where you can fill in your own expenses as you go. You might find that some of your expenses differ from the ones listed as examples in this book. That's okay! Make a line for those expenses and include them in your overall costs. The goal of filling in these lists is to get a sense of what you are spending your money on each month. On your worksheet, be sure to list only the expenses that are relevant to your spending plan.

At the top of the worksheet is a place for you to write how much you get paid each month. You must first have an accurate grasp on your means in order to live within them. To calculate this, look at your bank statements or paycheck stubs and determine the amount. Some people are paid twice per month while others are only once. These terms are typically outlined in your employment contract or employee handbook.

Next to the items in each list are lines for you to notate your expenses and a place for you to write how much each one costs, or what you can afford to spend on, each per month. After determining all of your monthly expenses for each list, add up their total costs and write it at the bottom of that list. This is your monthly total for that list. You will then subtract that total from your monthly income. This will be the total funds you have left available to allocate your next list, and so on and so forth.

There is a *Sample Spending Plan* on page 83. The numbers and expenses on it will likely be different than those of your plan; however, you will go through the same process to make yours.

"What I Need"—The Basics

First, you need to make sure that you are paying for everything you need to live as a functional member of society . . . also known as your basic, monthly living expenses. When you are starting out, this is where you will likely spend the majority of your income. In this list, be sure to include all of the things you need to pay for each month:

- Rent/Mortgage
- Cell Phone
- Gas
- Electric
- Internet
- Air conditioning
- Water
- Insurance:
     o Home/Renters
     o Auto
     o Life
     o Health
       If you get health insurance through your place of work, your employer will likely take this out of your paycheck before depositing it into your account. If not, be sure to plan for it!

Necessities

You might not purchase *all* of these items every month; however, it is important to save a little bit of money from each paycheck toward them. Trust me, there will come a time where you wear out your favorite work shoes and need to replace them or get sick and have to get a prescription filled.

- Food—dining out
- Medicine and doctors visits
- Cleaning supplies
- Pet food
- Clothing
- Other personal items

Emergency and Goals Savings Accounts

In saving up for emergencies and dreams alike, it's best to do as my dad said and "pay yourself first." Each month, put a little bit of money toward your future goals, emergency fund, and necessities. Even if it's only a small amount each month, over time that savings will add up.

As tempting as it will sometimes be to touch this fund for things other than emergencies or your goals, don't. Continue to save! You can never have too much money in reserve.

After you've accounted for everything classified as basic living expenses, add them all up and subtract this number from your total monthly income. This is how much money you have left to put toward your remaining two lists.

"Do I Have to"—The Creditors

When you see your bank account's balance on

payday, your first feeling is inevitably one of enthusiasm. That number is exciting, especially if the evening before you were deciding between fast-food dollar menus, packaged ramen, or canned soup for dinner. After the initial surge of delight, reality sets in and you start to wonder if you really have to pay all these bills with your hard-earned money. What are another few charges on the credit card if it allows you to revel in the feeling of having a bank account balance that doesn't cause you to cringe?

The truth is, if your goal is to be debt-free and not forever a slave to creditors then the answer is yes, you have to. You need to pay your debts first before you can spend money on things that you want to buy. The good news is that you can take back control of your cash flow and create a way to pay off what you owe as soon as possible! It will take discipline and time, but it is doable and most of all, worth it.

When you owe creditors money, they become the ones in control of where your cash is going. Spoiler alert, it is to them! Many loan and credit card companies exist solely to make money off the interest rates that they charge people on their loans. Each month you go without paying off your debt is another month that they profit off the interest you're paying them. If you run out of paycheck (money) before the end of your billing cycle and you still haven't paid your creditors, give them a call. It is essential to communicate with your creditors. They will work with you when you need it, but you must be the one to initiate that conversation. Don't bury your head in the sand and ignore them; they won't go away until they talk to you.

Take the initiative to communicate and assure them that they will get paid, even if it's not until your next paycheck.

Prov. 22:7b (NJKV): "The borrower is slave to the lender."

As reflected in the above verse, as long as you spend money you do not have, you are indebted to whoever lent it to you. Thus, this list is made up of all the debts you are currently paying down:

- Student Loans
- Other Loans
- Credit Card Debt

Add up the total of these monthly payments and subtract it from the amount you had left over after paying for your basic living expenses. This is what you have left to spend on things you want.

If you find yourself unable to make the minimum payments on your debts, you will need to find ways adjust your essential living expenses in order to do so. As wonderful as it might be to fantasize about a world without bills, the reality is that you cannot refuse to pay your debts!

"What I Want" – Your Lifestyle

Unfortunately, this list has to come last. You must take care of your obligations before spending money on the fun stuff. If you've accounted for all of the items on your other lists, use your remaining monthly income to spend on lifestyle expenses and to start accomplishing some of the short-term goals you established in chapter 2. For instance, if a goal of yours is to travel to Europe next summer, you may deposit extra money into your savings account each month with the idea that you'll slowly start to save up for the trip.

When making your "What I Want" list, be sure to put what's most important to you toward the top. Prioritize your list. Different leisure expenses might be

- Eating Out
- Memberships
    - o Gym (once you sign a contract for a membership, move this to fixed monthly expenses or "What I Need" list.
    - o Video-streaming services
    - o Magazine subscriptions
- Going to the movies
- Travel
- Salon/Beauty extras
- Shopping (other than for groceries)

If you find yourself with money remaining after accounting for the expenses on this list, add it to your savings accounts meant for emergencies and your long-term goals. When unexpected expenses come up, it's always better to be prepared than in a panic.

On the other hand, if you find yourself without any money to allocate toward this list after paying off your debts, you can do one of two things: find ways to earn a little extra income or cut back on your essential living expenses. You must continue paying your creditors what you owe them!

The Importance of Balance

Picture a three-legged stool. If one leg is shorter than the other two, the stool becomes unstable, and whoever sits on it will lose their balance. Your spending plan works in a similar fashion.

If you are consistently spending too much money on any one thing, you will drain your monetary resources and upset your financial balance. For example, if you continue to add to the list of people and entities that you owe, there will be less money left to pay for your essential living expenses and no money to fund your future goals. If no adjustments are made, you will become weighed down with debt, which makes it harder for you to reach your short- and long-term goals.

The secret to keeping your income harmoniously allocated between these three lists is simple: only live within your means. You don't have to live lavishly in order to enjoy life. In fact, there are many things you that you don't have to do that will help you save money:

- *You don't have to* pay full price for something. Buy sale items and clip coupons from your local newspaper or a vendor's website to use on groceries.

- *You don't have to* buy new. Buy used! There are many items that are perfectly good secondhand. Check out your local discount stores and mobile apps like Facebook Marketplace and OfferUp that allow you to browse what locals have for sale at significant discounts.

- *You don't have to* buy it now. Stop and think before you buy something. Do you really need it this second? If not, wait a couple weeks. If you still truly want it, can afford it, and it's still there, treat yourself. If not, you probably didn't need it anyway.

- *You don't have to* use a credit card. Pay cash whenever possible, and stick to your monthly spending plan! When emergencies arise, use the money in your emergency savings account; don't put the expenses on a credit card.

- *You don't have to* enhance your lifestyle when you have an increase in income. The current mindset is: "When I make more money I can buy a bigger house, a nicer car, a better wardrobe." To avoid creating a situation where you could more easily fall into debt, change your mindset to be: "When I make more money, I can save more money." Continue to live on the spending plan you put in place. Pay down your debts as quickly as possible and focus on saving money for your future.

Achieving balance in your spending takes time when you're starting out. If you have a setback, recognize it and get right back on track. Nobody's perfect. The key is to keep moving forward.

Mindset Matters

Being grateful for what you have is a very powerful way of thinking. It helps us find the positive in sometimes seemingly unfair situations. "Why me?"

becomes, "Whew, it could be a lot worse!"

Have you ever saved up enough money to buy that one, really awesome thing you've been dying to buy, and then *BOOM*, an unexpected expense pops up? Did you think, "Wow, I must have some bad luck?" I suggest you change your way of thinking to one of gratitude, and instead say, "Wow, I am thankful I have the money in savings to pay for this expense."

How your financial picture looks is a symptom of your mindset. Your values, commitment to stewardship, lifestyle choices, and how you spend your money all reflect your mindset. In addition to getting your finances in order, I deeply hope that this book brings you an awareness of your mindset. If you've gotten this far into the book, you either want to learn how to implement structure into your financial life, or something needs to change about your current financial picture. Both start with your mindset.

I remember when I realized the true power of shifting my perspective in this way. My husband and I were young parents saving money to update our flooring to hardwood in our first home. We had several setbacks and had to use some of that savings for new tires, then a new dryer, followed by a plumbing issue. Things we needed to take care of. The hardwoods were a lifestyle choice, not a necessity. Ultimately, we had to reset our goal of buying the hardwoods we wanted. While I was a little disappointed at first, I chose to look at the setback in a different way: to be grateful that we had the money to cover those expenses in our savings account and avoided going into credit card debt to take care of them.

dep - convenien
to track spending
· good for rewards

Using a credit card for emergencies is one of those things that seems like a good idea at first, but is actually a bad idea in the long run. Your savings account is what you should rely on when those unexpected expenses arise. When you use your credit card for emergencies, you begin a cycle of dependence on the credit card company. Instead, depend on yourself and your ability to pay your way by saving the proper amount to cover the unexpected expenses that will inevitably happen.

A Word on Debt

Let's take a minute to further address debt. This book is designed primarily to keep you from creating a lot of debt. There are certain types of debt many young adults find themselves in right out of college—student loans, moving expenses, a car down payment, etc. Having a little debt when you're starting out is okay. In fact, in this day and age, it's fairly normal. However, the goal is to quickly get out of the habit of having debt. It's one less thing to worry about and in the long-term will help you live a happier, more financially productive life. It's impossible to accomplish your long-term goals when you owe others money.

If you're reading this and feel that you are currently in a lot of debt, there are many great resources out there to help you pay down what you owe in an efficient and expedient way. A simple Google search will yield different plans and resources others have used to overcome their debt. You can also subscribe to my blog at www.sheriwilsonagency.com for additional ways to best manage your money.

Adjusting Your Plan

My dad used to always say, "Make your plan and work your plan." Your spending plan is meant to serve as a guide for how to allocate your income, keeping you on track to accomplish your short- and long-term goals, while also making sure your essential living expenses are taken care of.

As you acquire new goals and accomplish others, you will need to adjust your spending plan accordingly. This is also the case whenever something else in your financial life changes. For instance, whenever you move into a new place or upgrade to the faster wireless package, you will need to update your plan to account for the change in price.

If you stick with your plan and live within your means, adjusting along the way, you will live a financially stable, debt-free life.

Rules of Thumb

- Before you create a spending plan, it is imperative to know where you stand financially by calculating your net worth.

- When creating your spending plan, begin with your necessities and debts. What do I spend on keeping myself housed? Clothed and fed? Staying healthy? Getting to and from work? What do I owe others? After these essential expenses, the rest is fluff and optional. Be honest with yourself when you identify these necessary expenses

- Thirty percent of your gross monthly income is a

comfortable amount to allocate toward housing. This is a guideline; one can spend more or less, depending on your other fixed expenses like car payments, student loan payments, etc.

- Start by putting 10 percent of your monthly paycheck into a savings account. Pay yourself first.

- Once you've saved up $1,000 to $1,500 in your emergency savings account, open another savings account and start saving toward your other goals while continuing to deposit money into your emergency savings.

- Remember to keep the balance in your financial life by living within your means.

- Mindset is a powerful thing. If you find yourself thinking about all of the things you cannot buy, try switching your perspective to be grateful for all that you do have.

- You will need to adjust your plan as your financial situation changes, whether that be getting a new job with a new income, buying a new car, paying less on your phone bill each month, etc.

- Giving is a matter of the heart. Set up your financial plan and decide or pray about how much to give/tithe and then adjust your plan.

2Cor 9:7 (NKJV): "So let each one give as he purposes in his heart, not grudgingly or of necessity; for God loves a cheerful giver."

CHAPTER FOUR

I'M GLAD I DID – WORK YOUR PLAN AND MENTORS

With so many different decisions to make each day, it can be a struggle to balance meeting your current needs and having a little fun with saving up for the things you want to accomplish or buy. You have to pay for your basic living expenses and the debts that you owe, but it would be cruel not to allow yourself occasional indulgences. The ultimate goal is to learn how to allocate your money in such a way that you are able to enjoy a balanced lifestyle. You may not be able to buy and do everything that you want all the time. However, you shouldn't feel overly restricted or constantly worried about your money, either. To make sure you are achieving balance in your spending plan, it's crucial to do a yearly review of your finances.

Spending Plan Check-Ins

Reviewing your goals, net worth, and savings at least once a year allows you to make adjustments as things in your life change. It's good to note your progress on the items below in a notebook or spreadsheet somewhere that you can easily revisit them.

Goals

At the beginning of each calendar year, it is wise to take a look back at the previous year and review what you've accomplished. Assess each major area of your life: personal, family, professional, and financial. What went well and what didn't? Why?

Setting goals and reevaluating your progress toward reaching them is one of the best ways to immediately boost your sense of accomplishment. It feels good to look back over the last 365 days and see everything you checked off your list. Once you reach these goals, you are inspired to set new ones and continue these feelings of achievement.

While accomplishing goals is wonderful, it's crucial to also realize that pursuing one goal always affects your ability to achieve another. For example, focusing on advancing your career by putting in more hours at work will affect the amount of time you are able to devote to goals you have outside of work. That's why continually reassessing each goal's priority level is imperative. Ask yourself what you would like to accomplish in the upcoming year. Take a moment to also look back on your initial goals list. Are there any new ones to add? Any still on the list you no longer wish to accomplish? Out of all these goals, which take precedence this calendar year?

It is absolutely normal for your goals and priorities to change from year to year. You might even catch yourself drifting from the path you initially planned to be on. It happens. Recognize and adjust accordingly. Keep going.

Net Worth

Another great habit to get into is calculating your net worth on *at least* an annual basis. This will help you track the rates at which you are saving money and incurring debt, allowing you to adjust your spending plan if needed. Not saving enough? Decide what you can cut back on to save a bit more. Spending too much? Determine where and come up with a solution to spend less in that area! Math doesn't lie; trust your net worth statement to show you the truth about where you stand financially.

Savings

Finally, calculate the amount you were able to save within the last twelve months. Determine the total amount you had in your savings account(s) on January first of last year, and subtract it from the total amount you had in your savings accounts on January first of this year. That is how much you were able to save up over the course of the year. If your balance is zero, that means you spent it all. In this situation, don't beat yourself up. Simply, make adjustments for the upcoming year to build up your savings account. For ideas, you can refer back to the list in chapter 3 on how to adjust your lifestyle to save more money.

At the minimum, you should have six months worth of your expenses saved up in cash for unexpected emergencies. For instance, if you have a gap in employment, your expenses can be paid out of your cash reserve until you have a new job. Even after you have this amount saved up, continue saving! Stick to your spending plan and continue to put away a little bit each month. Slowly but surely, build up your reserve. You never know what curve balls you'll be thrown in life; however, having the money in your bank account to pay for something is a proven way to reduce the stress of many of life's crazy situations.

Proverbs 13:11 (NKJV): "Wealth gained hastily will dwindle, but whoever gathers little by little will increase it."

After reassessing your goals, net worth, and savings, you can make informed decisions on how your spending plan needs to be adjusted for the next year. Maybe you need to be saving a little more each month to make that bucket-list European vacation a reality. Perhaps you had a few unexpected expenses come up and need to focus on replenishing your savings or paying off a little debt. Whatever these adjustments are, they cannot be made until you are aware of them. The more in tune with your finances you are, the more control you have in preventing problems and accomplishing the goals you've set for yourself. Remember, you and you alone are responsible for making and working your plan. The closer you stick to it, the more

what & practices did I learn

you are able to accomplish!

My Own Lesson in Debt

While I was growing up, the advice I received from my parents regarding managing money was as follows:

1. Live within your means.

2. Pay yourself first.

3. Pay cash for what you buy.

4. Do not use credit cards.

All of this is sound advice, and I knew what I should do, but I wanted what I wanted. I worked part-time during high school and spent everything I earned on my lifestyle: buying new clothes, eating out with friends, going to the movies, or seeing my favorite band in concert. My parents covered living expenses, so I was free to spend on myself (very selfish, I know). While living at home in high school, it was great! When I moved out, however, it was a different story. I began to experience the consequences of my choices.

While in college, I didn't work my freshman and sophomore years, but I did work part-time my junior and senior years. My parents covered some of my expenses, and I covered others. College is a transition from being on your parents' payroll to gradually getting a job and living off your own paycheck.

By my senior year, I started receiving pre-approved credit card offers. I decided not to use a MasterCard or a Visa because not having to pay it off every month might cause me to run up a horrendous balance.

American Express, at the time, only had a card that required the balance to be paid every month. I thought applying for an American Express was a way for me to temper my spending. I got approved and got my card. As soon as it arrived in the mail, I felt I had just received free use of money. The first month I bought very little with my newfound money. However, by my sixth month, I was facing a bill of $600. I will never forget that amount and the feeling of sheer dread that came along with it. How was I supposed to pay back $600 when my part-time job only paid me roughly that amount per month AND take care of my other essential expenses? I had a problem: a deficit in my cash flow. At this point in my life I was not going to ask my parents to bail me out. They had helped me out enough and it was time for me to own my mistake and figure it out.

Being that I didn't have enough money to pay the balance, I called AMEX and explained my problem. They told me that it was okay, but that I could not use my card until the balance was paid. Oh, and that there was a penalty of $30 per month until the amount was paid. Wow! I didn't like those consequences and ended up learning my lesson the hard way because I did not listen to my parents. I didn't use my card for two months while I paid off the balance and vividly remember the feeling of utter relief when I finally did not owe AMEX any money.

I have credit cards now, but I use them; I don't let them use me. That is the essential difference. Think about that one for a minute. My knowledge about compounding interest and experience of being in and getting out debt taught me that I want to stay out of debt. Learn from the experiences of the people in your life that have gone before you. Speaking of . . .

Some of Your Best Resources

It is easy to overlook some of your most valuable resources—your elders. People in your life who have experienced so much more than you have. You have a wealth of experience available to you through your parents, grandparents, and mentors. Use it. Listen to their advice, their memories of the "good old days," and adventures in growing older.

You can become an expert on just about anything these days thanks to the Internet; however, perspective on an experience can only be gained by living it or listening to someone tell you about how they did.

A few years ago, in a moment of reflection, I realized my parents had been providing a wealth of knowledge and experience to me for all of my life. I'd been receiving it every time I asked, but I hadn't written any of it down. I felt a strong need to begin doing just that and decided to start documenting these words of wisdom that my parents gave me. I'll share how I started with my dad. I didn't want to overwhelm him by asking for everything at once, so I started by asking for just two of the best pieces of advice I could use. I asked him to base his answers on the following questions:

1. If he could go back and change something about how his life turned out by making a different decision, what would it be?

2. The most important piece of advice he could give to a young person just starting out. Something I could share with my children and grandchildren.

The first two pieces of advice I got were:

1. He wished he had found God at an earlier age. That it would have changed everything.

2. Understand the importance of compound interes; interest on savings and interest on debt.

Now, every time I see him I ask for more words of wisdom. Much of what I've written in this book came from my parents, my belief in God, my upbringing, and my own life experiences.

The lesson here is, do not be afraid or too proud to ask your parents, grandparents, or someone you consider a mentor whose advice you respect about their experiences. For example, How did they make major decisions in their life? What advice do they wish they had received when they were young? If they could go back and change any of the decisions they made, what would those be? Though challenging, what choices are they glad they made in spite of temptations to do otherwise?

Ask to hear their wisdom and listen to what they have to say. Write their lessons down. Learn from their successes and failures. You will gain so much insight into areas of your own life by taking the time to sit with them and learn about how they navigated these very same areas in theirs.

One of my favorite Bible verses is

Ecclesiastes 1:9 (NKJV): That which has been is what will be. That which is done is what will be done. And there is nothing new under the sun.

Everything that is happening to you has already happened to someone else, likely someone that you are rather close to. Take the time to ask those who came before you about their experiences. At best, it will save you a lot of trouble down the line. At worst, you'll have spent more time bonding with your loved ones. You have nothing to lose and everything to gain. When it comes to investing in your future, it's the wisest investment you could make. Don't let the opportunity pass while you still have the chance to seize it. You will be glad you did!

Call to Action!

If you get off track, know that you can always follow these steps and get back on the path toward a balanced financial life:

- Periodically do a review of the goals that you have achieved and ones that you still hope you will accomplish.

- Each year, recalculate your net worth and determine the amount that you have been able to save over the past 365 days.

- Based on these findings, adjust your spending plan so that you can continue to meet your goals or get back on track after a hiccup.

- Listen to the stories and advice of your parents,

grandparents, and mentors. Learn from their knowledge and experiences. Write the advice down so you can reflect upon it later. There are notes pages at the back of this book where you can document the nuggets of wisdom shared with you. Remember, there is nothing new in this life; it has all happened before!

- Write all of the above down and keep it somewhere safe. Being able to look back will allow you to celebrate where you've been and to continue moving forward with increasingly positive results.

- The time to start is now!

_____
_____
_____
_____
_____
_____
_____
_____
_____
_____
_____
_____
_____
_____
_____
_____
_____
_____
_____
_____
_____
_____
_____
_____
_____

CHAPTER 5

THERE IS ONE MORE THING—LIFE INSURANCE —UNDERSTANDING THE WHAT AND THE WHY

By the time you get to this part of the book, you are asking yourself how much more there is to know about money and finances. There is a lot, but not everything needs to be tackled at the same time. That is why you created your goals sheet and created your plan. Life insurance is just one more important piece to your financial puzzle for you to learn about early in life. And, now that you are putting the structure into your financial life, it's time to consider how to protect your loved ones and those assets you are working hard to create. Think about this: everyone is required to buy auto insurance, and if you have a mortgage on your home, you are required to buy home owners insurance. But life insurance is the most important type of insurance you could ever purchase because it protects the future of the most important thing in your life, and that is the future of your family. Even if you aren't married yet, you would be smart to consider your options for life insurance early when you are young, in good health, and the rates are the cheapest for you. We are going to talk life insurance basics and next steps. Let's get down to understanding the basics.

Key Terms You Need to Know

- **The Insured**: you, the life of the person insured by insurance company. If you pass away, the life insurance company pays your beneficiary.

- **Beneficiary**: your loved ones. The people most likely to be affected financially by your death. Whomever you want the insurance company to pay. If you are single, it may be your parents. If you are married, your spouse.

- **Life Insurance Company**: There are plenty out there. Start by asking your parents which kind of life insurance they have in place and which company they chose. Do a little research to make sure you buy from a financially strong company.

- **Death Benefit**: the amount of life insurance you buy. The amount the insurance company will pay your beneficiary in the event of your death.

- **Premium**: the payment for your life insurance

policy. The premium is based on the amount of death benefit and your health, or underwriting rating.

- **Underwriting**: the health assessment conducted by the insurance company to make sure you are a healthy candidate and a good risk to insure. A qualifying medical exam includes blood work, urine sample, blood pressure check, height and weight, and a list of prescriptions you take. A doctor's report is also ordered to examine your health history. Underwriting determines the rate or cost on insurance you will pay the insurance company. The insurance company has math wizards hired to determine if they are going to receive enough premium from your policy over time to pay for the death benefit if you were to pass away.

Why to Buy? Security for Your Family

I am unfortunate to be able to testify as to why to buy life insurance. In January 2017, my husband passed away unexpectedly. Just three years earlier, in 2014, we assessed our financial plan and discovered he was underinsured, so we doubled his life insurance policies. Being underinsured simply means that if our family lost his income, we would be in trouble financially. My security rested in being able to pay off our mortgage, pay for college for our three kids, and create a supplemental income stream to make up for his lost paycheck. The key is that we did our annual assessment, made adjustments, and reset our goals. I am glad we did because I am now secure. I'm not rich, but I'm secure and that is the why.

The best thing for you to do is discuss your options with your insurance agent, a financial planner, and your parents or mentor. Often times your auto and homeowners insurance agent sells life insurance or financial services and since you already have business with them, it's a good place to start.

The number one reason to buy life insurance is to replace lost income for the family. In the event of your death, the life insurance policy pays the beneficiary listed on the policy. The beneficiary will be given a lump sum payment to use as an income stream, fulfill debt obligations, pay for college for your children, pay off student loans, and cover any burial costs. Life insurance provides those you leave behind peace of mind that if you were gone, they would be fine financially.

There are two ways to buy life insurance: a term policy or a permanent policy. A term policy is very cost effective and you can usually buy a lot for very little. When you are young, your best bet is to buy as much as you can as cheap as you can. Most insurance companies sell terms of ten, twenty, or thirty years, and can start as low as $25,000 up to several million. Each company will have their own structure or products they offer.

The second option is a permanent policy. A permanent policy is usually more expensive because it has the ability to create a cash value, or an investment account. I like recommending a combination of insurance products for my financial planning clients. Buy a big term policy because it is cheap (think buying in bulk), and a small permanent policy to use as a tax-free savings account for ultra long-term goals. We are discussing the basics of insurance, and not going into the specifics of a policy, but I hope it gives you food for thought. Again, seek the advice of an insurance professional and your parents or mentor. You will be glad you did.

LIFE GOALS EXERCISE

What are my life goals?

List everything you would like to see happen in your life. Once you have your list, prioritize them on the timeline.

-

-

-

-

-

-

-

-

-

-

-

-

Short-, Medium- and Long-Term Goals

Short-term Goals: Six Months to One Year

Pay into a six-month cash reserve to use for emergencies. For example, new tires, replace a washer or dryer, or unforeseen dental or medical expenses. Better yet, pay into the beach vacation you will take next year.

Medium-term Goals: One to Three Years

Pay into a down payment on that new car. The goal is to pay cash for the car or lower the amount of money you borrow at an interest rate.

Long-term Goals: Three to Five Years

Pay into a down payment on your first home. A good rule of thumb is to save for 20 percent down payment for your home.

Ultra-long-term Goals: Five-Plus Years

Saving for the funds to start your own business or for future retirement income.

Six Month

•

•

Nine Months

•

•

One Year

-

-

Three Years

-

-

Five Years

-

-

Five-Plus Years

-

-

YOUR SPENDING PLAN

MONTHLY NET INCOME: _____

"What I Need" – The Basics

Necessities	Monthly Cost
Savings, 401k, and cash reserve	
Rent/Mortgage	
Home/Renters Insurance	
Car Payment	
Health Insurance (if not deducted from paycheck)	
Life Insurance	
Auto Insurance	
Internet	
Gas/Electric	
Water	
Phone	
Groceries	
Clothing or Personal Items (Salon/Beauty)	
Total "What I Need"	

"What I Owe" – Do I Have To?

Debt	Balance	Monthly Payment
Mortgage		
Auto Loans		
Credit Cards		
Financial Institutions: Student Loans		
Taxes Owed		
Money Owed to Others		
Total "What I Owe"		

"What I Need" – "What I Owe" = "What I Want Fund"

"What I Need" total	
- "What I Owe" total	-
Total available to spend "What I Want"	

"What I Want" – Lifestyle

The Fun Stuff

Total "What I Want"	
Dining Out	
Gym Membership (when you sign a contract memberships move to the necessities list)	
Entertainment	
Other	
BALANCE – anything left, bank it into a savings account toward future goals	

Microsoft® Excel® has money management templates, or you can find money management or budgeting apps for your phone or online.

YOUR SPENDING PLAN—SAMPLE

MONTHLY NET INCOME: $3,500

"What I Need" – The Basics

Necessities	Monthly Cost
Savings, 401k, and cash reserve	$450
Rent/Mortgage	$1,000
Home/Renters Insurance	$20
Car Payment	See "What I Owe" – Auto Loans
Health Insurance (if not deducted from paycheck)	$85
Life Insurance	$55
Auto Insurance	$175
Internet	$80
Gas/Electric	$55
Water	$25
Phone	$65
Groceries	$250
Clothing or Personal Items (Salon/ Beauty)	$200
Total "What I Need"	**$2,460**

"What I Owe" – Do I Have To?

Debt	Balance	Monthly Payment
Mortgage	Renting for this example	
Auto Loans	$8,500	$250
Credit Cards	$3,000	Min. Payment $180
Financial Institutions: Student Loans	$65,000	$350
Taxes Owed		
Money Owed to Others		
Total "What I Owe"		**$780**

"What I Need" – "What I Owe" = "What I Want" Fund

Monthy Net Income	$3,500
- "What I Need" total	- $2,460
- "What I Owe" total	- $780
Total available to spend "What I Want"	$260

"What I Want" – Lifestyle

The Fun

Total "What I Want"	$260
Dining Out	- $100
Gym Membership (when you sign a contract, memberships move to the necessities list)	- $40
Entertainment (movies, golf)	- $80
Other	
BALANCE – anything left, bank it into a savings account toward future goals	$40

Microsoft® Excel® has money management templates, or you can find money management or budgeting apps for your phone or online.

YOUR NET WORTH STATEMENT
Assets – Liabilities

Monthly Gross Income: $_____

Annual Gross Income: $_____

Assets – "What I Own"

Property	Value
Home	
Other Real Estate	
Checking	
Savings	
401k and IRA	
Investment Accounts	
Cash-Value Life Insurance	
Auto	
Money Owed to You	
Total	

Liabilities – "What I Owe"

Who I Owe	Balance
Mortgage	
Auto Loans	
Credit Cards	
Financial Institutions/Student Loans	
Taxes Owed	
Money Owed to Others	
Total	

Net Worth – "What I'm Worth" (financially speaking)

Assets	
Liabilities	
Net Worth Total	

_____

_____

_____

_____

_____

_____

_____

_____

_____

_____

_____

_____

_____

_____

_____

_____

_____

_____

_____

_____

_____

_____

_____

NUGGETS OF
SHARED WISDOM

_____

_____

_____

_____

_____

_____

_____

_____

_____

_____

_____

_____

_____

_____

_____

_____

_____

_____

_____

_____

_____

_____

_____

_____

Nuggets of Shared Wisdom

_____

_____

_____

_____

_____

_____

_____

_____

_____

_____

_____

_____

_____

_____

_____

_____

_____

_____

_____

_____

_____

_____

_____

_____

NUGGETS OF
SHARED WISDOM

_____
_____
_____
_____
_____
_____
_____
_____
_____
_____
_____
_____
_____
_____
_____
_____
_____
_____
_____
_____
_____
_____
_____

NUGGETS OF
SHARED WISDOM

_____

_____

_____

_____

_____

_____

_____

_____

_____

_____

_____

_____

_____

_____

_____

_____

_____

_____

_____

_____

_____

_____

_____

NUGGETS OF
SHARED WISDOM

_____

_____

_____

_____

_____

_____

_____

_____

_____

_____

_____

_____

_____

_____

_____

_____

_____

_____

_____

_____

_____

_____

Nuggets of
Shared Wisdom

_____

_____

_____

_____

_____

_____

_____

_____

_____

_____

_____

_____

_____

_____

_____

_____

_____

_____

_____

_____

_____

_____

_____

NUGGETS OF SHARED WISDOM

_____

_____

_____

_____

_____

_____

_____

_____

_____

_____

_____

_____

_____

_____

_____

_____

_____

_____

_____

_____

_____

_____

_____

_____

CPSIA information can be obtained
at www.ICGtesting.com
Printed in the USA
FFOW05n0914031217